1001 WAYS TO
FRIENDSHIP

D1375188

ARCTURUS

With special thanks to Anne Moreland

Arcturus

This edition published in 2015 by Arcturus Publishing Limited
26/27 Bickels Yard, 151–153 Bermondsey Street,
London SE1 3HA

ISBN: 978-1-84858-549-2
AD002246UK

Printed in China

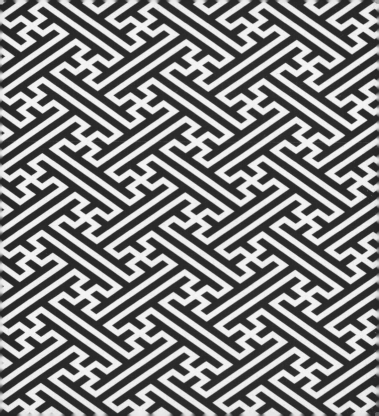

Contents

Introduction

The bond of friendship is one that is often overlooked, yet is one of the most important human relationships. It is a deep recognition of our common humanity, and can be a source of great joy, from childhood through to adulthood. A true friend can share fun and laughter in happy times; provide reassurance and comfort in times of distress; give advice when we find ourselves troubled; tolerate our moods with patience; gently criticize our faults; and be a true companion on life's pathway.

Finding a good friend is an extraordinary piece of luck in life, and one that we should never take for granted. It's important to realize that friendships, like all relationships, must be nurtured; small acts, like helping out with chores, remembering birthdays, wishing good luck for important new challenges, and so on, are all ways of showing your friends that you care.

A recent survey showed that most people, of whatever age, number their close friends on one hand. We may have five hundred friends on Facebook, but when it comes down to it, most of us have only between one and five friends we can really count on. This little book will help you to see why those few friends are so important, and why – on a bigger scale – the natural bond of selfless love between human beings that we call friendship is so essential in building communities, societies, bonds between nations, and hence, a better world for all of us.

What is Friendship?

Friendship is one of the most precious kinds of love, but it is a relationship whose importance is often overlooked. What is a true friend, and how does friendship differ from romantic and other kinds of attachment?

The art of friendship is like any other art: it must be practised with love, care, and tenderness if it is to thrive.

The gift of friendship is the greatest gift a person can ever possess.

Take care of your friends, and your friends will take care of you.

Friendship is a sheltering tree.
Samuel Taylor Coleridge

Friendship isn't a big thing – it's a million little things.

From quiet homes and first beginning
Out to the undiscovered ends
There's nothing worth the wear of winning
But laughter and the love of friends.

Hilaire Belloc

Friendship is love for its own sake.

A true friend is someone you can trust implicitly, at all times.

Friendship demands:
Honesty
Trustworthiness
Tolerance
Loyalty
Care
Concern
… and last, but by no means least, being able to have fun together.

The greatest blessings in life are love, peace, freedom, and friendship.

Friendship is a flower that grows in the most unexpected places.

When you meet new people, don't jump to conclusions. Sometimes, a person you take an immediate dislike to may turn out to become a firm friend.

No distance of place or lapse of time can lessen the friendship of those who are thoroughly persuaded of each other's worth.

Robert Southey

Only as we grow older do we really appreciate the gift of having true, loyal, and loving friends.

The key of love opens the door of friendship.

A friend is the first person you want to call when you hear good news.

Making a new friend can take time and tact. 'Will you be my friend?' is a question only heard in the playground – or on social networking sites!

Friends are more important than lovers. Lovers come and go, but a good friend will stick with you throughout your life.

Friendship means:
- **remembering to call when things go wrong**
- **celebrating when things go right**
- **laughing when things go awry**
- **listening when things get difficult**
- **helping when things need doing**

If you have even one friend you can trust completely, and rely on absolutely, then you are the luckiest person in the world.

Our friends are those who will accept our faults, and celebrate our strengths. But, however close they are, we have to be careful not to take them for granted.

19

If friends live far away, make an effort to keep in touch. A simple Christmas or birthday card, a phone call, or a letter, will help to keep your friendship strong.

'Tis the privilege of friendship to talk nonsense, and have her nonsense respected.

Charles Lamb

Friends are faithful, fun, foolish; and, sadly, sometimes few and far between.

Some people weave cotton into the fabric of our lives; some weave gold thread. Both contribute to make the tapestry beautiful and unique.

Business, you know, may bring money, but friendship hardly ever does. *Jane Austen*

You realize you have made a friend when silence falls between you, and it doesn't make either of you feel uncomfortable.

To take stock of yourself, look at your friends.

One of life's greatest pleasures is reminiscing about past times, good or bad, with an old and trusted friend. It helps us to know that there are others who remember our lives, have shared them with us, and continue to do so.

A true friendship is as wise as it is tender. The parties to it yield implicitly to the guidance of their love, and know no other law nor kindness.

Henry David Thoreau

There is no laughter like the laughter of old friends.

Friendship is one of life's greatest joys.

As widowers proverbially marry again, so a man with the habit of friendship always finds new friends.
George Santayana

The single most important acquisition for a happy life is that of a friend.

A friend is the person who will help you with the dullest of chores, and make them seem fun.

Be civil to all; sociable to many; familiar with few; friend to one; enemy to none.

Benjamin Franklin

Friends of the right kind will help you far more than money or success ever will.

A friendship with no trust is like a cell phone with no network coverage. All you can do is play games!

The world is so empty if one thinks only of mountains, rivers, and cities; but to know someone who thinks and feels with us, and who, though distant, is close to us in spirit, this makes the earth for us an inhabited garden.

Johann Wolfgang von Goethe

A good friend is cheaper than therapy.

Giving all, expecting nothing: the mark of a loyal friend.

A friend is someone you can be silly with, and never feel embarrassed for a moment.

A friend who is far away is sometimes much nearer than one who is at hand. Is not the mountain far more awe-inspiring and more clearly visible to one passing through the valley than to those who inhabit the mountain? *Khalil Gibran*

Friends are kisses blown to us by angels.

Friendship is the source of the greatest pleasures, and without friends even the most agreeable pursuits become tedious.
Thomas Aquinas

The worst affliction any human being can have is to know no one who cares.

Friendships change as the years go by. At times, as circumstances alter, you may be close; at other times, less so. If you make the effort to continue to remain friends, despite these ups and downs, you may find that eventually you will become as close as you ever were again.

The best way to mend a broken heart is time, and girlfriends.

Gwyneth Paltrow

If we cannot be ourselves with our friends, we cannot be ourselves at all.

Before borrowing money from a friend, decide which you need most.

A friend invites honesty; accept the invitation.

Romantic love is turbulent passion; friendship calm delight.

To have a true friend is a great honour, so be sure not to take it for granted.

A lover, a child, a parent, a partner; all these have their place in life, and without them we would be bereft. But a friend beside you, calm, trusting, and loyal, can be just as important.

Do not keep on with a mockery of friendship after the substance is gone – but part, while you can part friends. Bury the carcass of friendship; it is not worth embalming.

William Hazlitt

A friend endowed with seven qualities is worth associating with. Which seven?
- He gives what is hard to give
- He does what is hard to do
- He endures what is hard to endure
- He reveals his secrets to you
- He keeps your secrets
- When misfortunes strike, he doesn't abandon you
- When you're down and out, he doesn't look down on you

Buddha

Love; respect; loyalty; empathy; humour: the gifts friends give each other every day.

The essence of friendship is that you can talk about anything, knowing that your secrets are safe, and will be carefully guarded from idle gossip.

We don't always seek advice from our friends: sometimes we just want someone to listen.

Heavy is the heart that cannot unburden itself to a friend.

Wearing a friendship bracelet tells the world you are friends; but true friends need no such outward sign of loyalty.

If your paths do not cross daily, monthly, or even yearly, you will have to make an effort to keep a friend. Try to do so; in the long term, once your lives have become less busy, you may find you have more opportunity to spend time with each other.

The first green shoots of spring; a summer rose in full bloom; the changing colours of autumn; a fall of soft white snow: what are these joys if we have no friend to share them with?

A loyal friend laughs at your jokes when they're not so good, and sympathizes with your problems when they're not so bad.
Arnold H. Glasgow

As well as family ties, human beings need the close companionship of friends that they choose for themselves, out of the many people that they encounter throughout their lives.

Opposites attract. This can be true of friends, as well as lovers.

Friendship is: a quiet chat over morning coffee; a long walk in the park on a sunny afternoon; a quick bite to eat at lunchtime on a busy weekday; a laugh and a joke over an evening drink in a crowded bar; talking far into the night after coming home from a party; a late-night telephone call when times get tough.

More than your money and possessions, friends are your greatest asset in life.

I count myself in nothing else so happy
As in a soul remembering my good friends.
William Shakespeare

A friendly, open, positive attitude to those you meet along life's way will always stand you in good stead. In most cases, you will find it an effective antidote to hostility, rudeness, and bad manners.

Happiness is, in most of us, dependent on having friends; not a large number, but at least one or two.

Remember, no one friend can be everything to you. There are bound to be disappointments and differences that arise between you at times. Forgiving and forgetting these is part of friendship.

When friendship dies, it's not always a tragedy. Sometimes, in order to grow and change, friends need to go their separate ways. But their friendship will always be a part of each of them.

True happiness is of a retired nature, and an enemy to pomp and noise; it arises, in the first place, from the enjoyment of one's self, and, in the next, from the friendship and conversation of a few select companions.

Joseph Addison

Nobody teaches you how to have, and keep, a friend. It is something you must learn for yourself.

Sometimes, it takes the arrival of a new friend in our lives to show us who we really are.

When you prosper, you will find many friends; in times of adversity, most of them will disappear. The few who remain are the ones to cherish throughout your life.

Be kind; be loyal; be tolerant; be open; be honest; be thoughtful; be silly; be serious; be a friend.

There are only two people who can tell you the truth about yourself – an enemy who has lost his temper and a friend who loves you dearly.

Antisthenes

Friendship is a plant that must be often watered.

True friendship is not based on glamour or success. It arises spontaneously, between two people who take a liking to each other, for no reason other than that.

A good friend gives you courage to face life's challenges.

The best preservative to keep the mind in health is the faithful admonition of a friend.
Francis Bacon

Nobody goes out of the house in the morning with the specific intention of making friends; but being well disposed to your fellow human being, and trying to connect with the people you meet as you go through your day, is a good way to start.

And in the sweetness of friendship let there be laughter and sharing of pleasures, for in the dew of little things the heart finds its meaning and is refreshed. *Khalil Gibran*

Friendship is a matter of sticking by each other, come what may, through thick and thin.

Say 'thank you' to your friend, often, and from the heart. However close you are to each other, nobody likes to be taken for granted.

When you are irritated with friends, ask yourself, do I ever behave in a way that irritates them? You'll probably find yourself answering yes.

In friendship, as in the rest of life, being right is often not as important as being kind.

The person who tries to live alone will not succeed as a human being. His heart withers if it does not answer another heart. His mind shrinks away if he hears only the echoes of his own thoughts and finds no other inspiration. *Pearl S. Buck*

You may disagree with your friends; you may not understand the choices they make; you may find their partners, children, or relatives irritating; you may find yourself impatient with some of their less attractive traits; yet, you must remember, their friendship is precious to you, and these difficulties must be overcome.

To have even one good friend in life is a blessing.

The glory of friendship is not the outstretched hand, nor the kindly smile, nor the joy of companionship; it is the spiritual inspiration that comes to one when he discovers that someone else believes in him and is willing to trust him.
Ralph Waldo Emerson

Throughout your life, you will make many acquaintances; you will make much fewer friends. It's important to know the difference.

Our friends help us to measure, and value, the stages we go through in life: the energy of childhood; the excitement of teenage years; the ambition of young adulthood; the maturity of middle age; and finally, the tranquillity of old age.

Friendship is like an olive tree: it shades us in summer; provides fruit for us in winter; shows us sweet flowers; and has leaves that are evergreen. It is firmly planted in the soil, and however strong the winds may blow, it cannot be uprooted.

No love, no friendship can cross the path of our destiny without leaving some mark on it forever.

François Mauriac

**If fortune does not favour you,
your faithful friends will have to do.**

Treasure your friends, for they are the ones who bring light into your life.

Trouble is a sieve through which we sift our acquaintances. Those too big to pass through are our friends.

Arlene Francis

To be capable of steady friendship or lasting love, are the two greatest proofs, not only of goodness of heart, but of strength of mind. *William Hazlitt*

Friendship is a question of making allowances for each other; overlooking faults, and forgiving mistakes.

A man who is rich but has no friends is more to be pitied than envied.

What I cannot love, I overlook.

Anaïs Nin

We learn our virtues from our friends who love us; our faults from the enemy who hates us. We cannot easily discover our real character from a friend. He is a mirror, on which the warmth of our breath impedes the clearness of the reflection. *Jean Paul Richter*

Friendship is the most selfless form of love.

Nothing makes the earth seem so spacious as to have friends at a distance; they make the latitudes and longitudes. *Henry David Thoreau*

Four-legged friends are the best companions you can have; you can talk to them about anything, and they won't give their own opinion, or answer back!

Parents and children can form friendships with each other; on the other hand, they may not be temperamentally suited to do so. If you find friendship in your family, enjoy it; if not, accept that they love you, and you love them, which should be enough.

A garden is a friend that you can visit whenever you feel like it.

Good friends give advice; best friends listen.

If we would build on a sure foundation in friendship, we must love friends for their sake, rather than our own.

Charlotte Brontë

The Art of Friendship

How is a friendship nourished over the years? Are friends that last a lifetime the most important ones in our lives, and how do we react when a friendship ends? Also, what are the qualities needed to find and keep a good friend?

Friendship is an art which, like any other, must be practised and refined throughout a lifetime.

In your old age, you will reap the benefit of friends that you have been loyal to over many years.

What is a friend?

- The person you consult about your problems, whether large or small
- The person you celebrate with when something wonderful happens
- The person whose shoulder you cry on when something upsets you
- The person you complain to about the little things in life that bug you
- The person you trust with your secrets
- The person you miss when they're away on holiday
- The person whose birthday you always remember
- The person who has the nerve to tell you when you make a fool of yourself
- The person you still love when they do the same

As time passes, we often become separated from our friends. They go to live in different cities, or countries, start families, make new friends. If you want to keep in touch, make sure you organize visits occasionally if possible – travel to where they live, have them to stay, or meet somewhere halfway between your homes.

A close friend is always with you. Even if you fall out, or lose touch over time, he or she will continue to remain in your memory, marking your life.

Friendship can be a demanding occupation. If you have a lot of friends, it may be that you're not giving as much as you should to each of them.

There is no hope of joy except in human relations.

Antoine de Saint-Exupéry

Friends are made, not born.

Friendship is a rose without a thorn.

Never trust friends who are indiscreet with your secrets. Even if they do not mean to be malicious, they won't be able to stop themselves gossiping about your intimate revelations.

Friends are the flowers in the garden of life.

A new friend is always a mystery. He or she may turn out to be a friend for life, or just passing your way.

There is magic in the memory of schoolboy friendships. *Benjamin Disraeli*

A cheerful friend is like the dawning of a sunny day: a joy to everyone.

Most friends have a great deal in common; but that doesn't go for all friends. Sometimes, close friends can be like chalk and cheese.

It's always TEA time with good friends: tolerance, equality, affection.

73

Close friends are like singers in harmony;
you can't tell one voice from the other.

A firm friend will help
you through times
that are good, and
times that are bad;
times that are happy,
and times that are sad.

Without wearing any mask we are conscious of, we have a special face for each of our friends. *Oliver Wendell Holmes*

Make time for your friends. They are the people who share your life, and help you to savour it.

Ask yourself, do you care for your friends as much as they do for you? Do you show them, in little ways, that you remember them? Hopefully, the answer is 'Yes!' If it isn't, try to make amends.

It's good to have old friends, but always be prepared to make new ones.

Children often become upset when their school friends move away. It's easy for parents to worry about that. But what matters is that a child knows how to make and value friends, not that they keep the same friends throughout their lives.

A friend is a person who allows us the freedom to explore our own identity. And vice versa.

When you choose your friends, don't be short-changed by choosing personality over character.

W. Somerset Maugham

The only unsinkable ship is friendship.

Friendship is an essential part of a rich, full life; but solitude has its place, too.

A friend is the person who is there for you when he'd rather be somewhere else.

Regard everyone as a friend until they prove otherwise.

Friendships are fragile, and need to be handled with care, just like any other valuable object.

Never play second fiddle to a friend, unless you've consciously chosen to do.

Each person you meet may be a doorway to a new world.

If you make a fool of yourself, your friend will understand that your idiocy is a temporary condition.

Laughter is the shortest distance between friends.

Mighty proud am I that I am able to have a spare bed for friends.
Samuel Pepys

There are friends who find time for you in their diaries; and friends who don't consult their diaries before arranging to see you. The second category you can identify as your closest friends.

Friendship nourishes the spirit.

Some people have a talent for friendship; others must learn the art painstakingly, through trial and error, as they go through life.

A good friend is a family member that destiny forgot to supply you with.

The greatest success of your life is to have one or two really good friends.

We are all angels with only one wing; we can only fly by embracing each other...

The best antiques are your old friends.

I have friends in overalls whose friendships I would not swap for the favour of the kings of the world.
Thomas Edison

A shoulder to cry on, and an ear to listen with, are the essential qualities of a good friend.

You are only complete when you have a true friend, someone who will share your joys and sorrows throughout life, and stand by you until the last.

Imagine being in a beautiful, sunny garden with a wonderful view. There is a warm swimming pool waiting for you to step into, soft music playing in the background, and a great selection of food and drink at the bar. You have everything you need to relax and enjoy yourself. What would make the scene complete? Friends, of course – people to share it all with.

Scatter the seeds of friendship, and you will reap joy.

Writing a diary, describing your intimate thoughts, is a kind of friendship – with yourself.

87

How does a friendship begin? A few chance meetings; friends in common; shared interests, in work or at play; invitations out, at first in groups, then just the two of you; talking to each other, generally, then more intimately; helping each other out with a task or problem; and suddenly you find you've made a friend.

Reach for a friend's hand, and you touch his heart.

But friendship is precious, not only in the shade, but in the sunshine of life, and thanks to a benevolent arrangement, the greater part of life is sunshine. *Thomas Jefferson*

Social friends expect you to entertain them; real friends put up with you even when you're a bore.

Without good friends to advise and calm, many turbulent romances would never get off the ground.

If you can't tell a friend the truth, the best option is to remain silent. Telling lies tends to lead to trouble, because lies are usually found out in the end.

Birds of a feather stick together.

There is nothing so well worth having as friends.

Don't ask too much of your friends – except occasionally, in emergencies.

Friends are destiny's apology for annoying family members.

It is not flesh and blood but the heart that makes us fathers and sons.

Friedrich Schiller

A successful marriage or partnership is immeasurably helped by having supportive family and friends.

A little Consideration, a little Thought for Others, makes all the difference. *Winnie the Pooh*

Life should be fortified by many friendships.

When you meet a friend in a foreign place, it's surprising how much closer the two of you feel.

The mere fact of sharing a common past brings old friends, who may have their differences, together again.

It's easy to fall out with a friend; harder to fall in with them afterwards.

A good friend will help you in times of trouble. But if your life is a constant drama, he or she may tire of doing so.

Friendships often start when we realize, for the first time, that someone else feels exactly the same way we do.

Making childish jokes is something we can only do in the company of our dearest friends.

Sometimes, after a tiff with a friend, you may need to take a step back and give yourselves a little space. But don't let the cooling-off period last too long, or the friendship might grow colder than you wished.

Friendship is giving, and forgiving.

Me, too, thy nobleness has taught
To master my despair;
The fountains of my hidden life
Are through thy friendship fair.
Ralph Waldo Emerson

Best friends go from being friends to being family.

Love for a friend can be deeper, and last longer, than romantic love.

Be thankful for one true friend in your life; many people have no such friend.

When friends first meet, they often talk a lot, so that they can get to know each other. Later, they often don't need to talk much, because they know each other so well.

Father, mother, brother, sister: my best friend.

Don't spend time with people who belittle your ambitions. You need friends who believe in you, so that you can start to believe in yourself.

Life is partly what you make it, and partly what it is made by the friends we choose.
Tennessee Williams

A smile costs nothing, but it has great value.

Friendship is sometimes a balance between giving, and withholding, advice.

Health is the first good lent to men;
A gentle disposition then;
Next, to be rich by no by-ways
Lastly, with friends t'enjoy our days.

Robert Herrick

There is no formula for friendship, because all friendships are different.

No one with true friends feels worthy of them.

There are some friends whose advice you should take seriously; others who, with the best will in the world, will not be very thoughtful. The trick is to distinguish between the two kinds.

It requires confidence to extend the hand of friendship. But remember, someone has to make the first move, and even if you are rejected, you'll be the one who had the courage to put yourself on the line.

It is said that too many cooks spoil the broth; but a single, trusted friend to help you in the kitchen when you have a big meal to prepare is actually a great asset.

But if the while I think on thee, dear friend All losses are restored and sorrows end.

William Shakespeare

In friendship, quality is more important than number.

Could we but draw back the curtain
That surrounds each other's lives
See the naked heart and spirit;
Know what spur the action gives;
Often we would find it better,
Purer than we think we would
We would love each other better
If we only understood.

Laughing over one's youthful foolishness with an old friend is one of the best ways to spend one's declining years.

In everyone's lives, there are worrying, even frightening, times. That is when the calm voice of a friend, standing right beside you, can offer reassurance until the problem or danger is past.

What is it that your friends like about you? And what is it that you like about them? If you think about it, you'll find some aspects of yourselves that are just the same, and others that are completely different.

Friendship is born at that moment when one says, 'What, you too? I thought I was the only one.' *C.S. Lewis*

There are many kinds of love, but the three greatest are: romantic love, the love of a parent for a child, and the love between friends.

Your family is given to you by destiny; your friends, by chance.

In times of trouble, a good friend must be our first port of call.

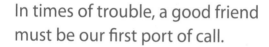

Only a life lived for others is worth living.

Albert Einstein

Friendship is a question of timing:
A time to warn; a time to argue;
a time to hold your peace;
A time to help; a time to comfort;
and a time to repair the damage
when it is done.

Friendship should never be a means to an end. If it is, it is not true friendship.

Give your friend the most precious gift you have to offer. Your time.

Think back to how you made your closest friends. Chances are, there'll be one you didn't like when you first met; another that you took an instant shine to; and another that you didn't notice for a while, until you'd met quite a few times.

How do children learn to make friends? Through the joy and fun of playing together. Make sure that, as an adult, you don't forget to play together sometimes.

Borrow money from a bank, rather than from your friends.

Life is mostly froth and bubble
Two things stand like stone
Kindness in another's trouble
Courage in your own.

Adam Lindsay Gordon

As we go through life, our friends change. Sometimes, the changes are so great it's hard to find anything in common with each other. Be patient, though, and after a while the changes won't seem as important as the things that haven't changed a bit.

There's nothing like a good laugh with friends who don't care how ridiculous you are.

We can see the faults in our friends quite clearly; in ourselves, less so.

115

The seven rules of friendship:
- **Keep your appointments**
- **Remember birthdays**
- **Enquire after relatives**
- **Don't borrow money, and if you do, pay it back quickly**
- **Listen more than you speak**
- **Don't criticize your friend's partner, children, or family**
- **Be discreet**

I wonder what Piglet is doing, said Pooh,
I wish I were there to be doing it too.

Winnie the Pooh

Blood is thicker than water. But it can also be more cloying.

From time to time, you may have to tell your friend a few white lies. If that's the case, remember, being kind is sometimes more important than being brutally honest.

There are few human beings in the world who do not wish, in their hearts, that they had many good friends.

Solitude and friendship are not incompatible; in a full, happy life there must be a proper balance between the two.

Be slow to make friends; and quick to keep them.

Never break a promise to a friend.

A true friend does not envy your success, or despise your failure.

The kindest word in all the world is the unkind word not said.

When you talk too much, are you drowning out the possibility of listening to your friend's story?

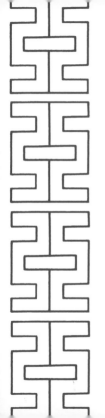

There is no greater loan than a sympathetic ear.

Frank Tyger

Friends sometimes hurt each other; when that happens, they must learn to speak frankly, then forgive and forget.

We all have different kinds of friends; some, like champagne, make us giggle; others, like black coffee, stimulate us; and yet others, like chamomile tea, help us to calm down after an anxious day.

In a soulmate we find, not company, but completed solitude.

Robert Brault

Have you ever seen two old people sitting on a park bench laughing together over some private joke, and thought, I hope I have someone like that as a friend when I'm their age?

We all need to be alone sometimes; but none of us need, or want, to be lonely at any time.

The sweetness of a true friend's smile, their kiss of gratitude for a small favour or gift, is one of life's greatest joys.

Man loves company, even if it is only that of a small, burning candle.

Georg Lichtenberg

Don't be envious of a popular, successful person who appears to have many friends; when times get hard, he or she may not find one true friend among them.

Everybody likes people with a cheerful disposition. But if it doesn't come naturally, don't force it. Instead, keep an open mind, listen to what others have to say, and you may find your mood lifts, all by itself.

Guard well within yourself that treasure, kindness. Know how to give without hesitation, how to lose without regret, how to acquire without meanness.

George Sand

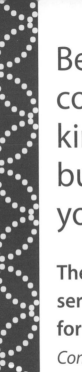

Behave with consideration and kindness to all, but especially to your friends.

There is one word that may serve as a rule of practice for one's life: reciprocity.

Confucius

The Guides

Many people who have made their mark on the world have offered advice on the question of friendship. Here are some of their thoughts, along with those of folklore and legend from a variety of cultures.

Friendship is love without his wings.

Lord Byron

Friendship is the golden thread that ties the heart of all the world.

Friendship is one mind in two bodies.
Mencius

Think where man's glory
most begins and ends
And say my glory was
I had such friends.

W.B. Yeats

Don't walk in front of me, I may not follow.
Don't walk behind me, I may not lead.
Walk beside me and be my friend.

Albert Camus

It is a good thing to be rich,
and a good thing to be strong;
but it is a better thing to be
loved by many friends.

Euripides

Friends are relatives you make for yourself.

Eustache Deschamps

The best mirror is an old friend.

George Herbert

What do we live for if not to make life less difficult for each other?

George Eliot

Each friend represents a world in us, a world possibly not born until they arrive. *Anaïs Nin*

No man is useless while he has a friend.
Robert Louis Stevenson

Some people go to priests, others to poetry; I to my friends.
Virginia Woolf

Time makes friendship stronger, but love weaker.

Jean de la Bruyère

Secrecy is the chastity of friendship.
Jeremy Taylor

Few things tend more to alienate friendship than a want of punctuality in our engagements. I have known the breach of a promise to dine or sup to break up more than one intimacy.

William Hazlitt

The best time to make friends is before you need them.

Ethel Barrymore

Friendship is a battered old bus, not a bright, shiny sportscar.

My best friend is the one who brings out the best in me. *Henry Ford*

The greatest sweetener of human life is friendship. To raise this to the highest pitch of enjoyment, is a secret which but few discover.
Joseph Addison

Friendship is a common belief in the same fallacies, mountebanks, and hobgoblins.

H.L. Mencken

Advice is like snow; the softer it falls, the longer it dwells upon, and the deeper it sinks into the mind.

Samuel Taylor Coleridge

Those friends thou hast, and their adoption tried,

Grapple them to thy soul with hoops of steel;

But do not dull thy palm with entertainment

Of each new-hatch'd, unfledged comrade.

William Shakespeare

Make new friends, and keep the old
One is silver, the other gold.

If you judge people, you have no time to love them.

Mother Teresa

My friends are my estate.

Emily Dickinson

The friend is the man who knows all about you, and still likes you.
Elbert Hubbard

Friendship is the shadow of the evening, which increases with the setting sun of life.
Jean de la Fontaine

A friend is the person who comes round to help you clear up after the party.

No man is an island entire of itself; every man
is a piece of the continent, a part of the main…
any man's death diminishes me,
because I am involved in mankind.
And therefore never send to know for whom
the bell tolls; it tolls for thee.

John Donne

A friend may well be reckoned the masterpiece of nature. *Ralph Waldo Emerson*

Your lost friends are not dead, but gone before, advanced a stage or two upon that road which you must travel in the steps they trod. **Aristophanes**

'Stay' is a charming word in a friend's vocabulary. *Louisa May Alcott*

I was angry with my friend
I told my wrath, my wrath did end.
I was angry with my foe
I told it not, my wrath did grow.

William Blake

The feeling of friendship is like that of being comfortably filled with roast beef; love, like that of being enlivened with champagne.
Samuel Johnson

A good friend is your closest family member.

Constant use will not wear ragged the fabric of friendship. *Dorothy Parker*

A friend is a person who knows all about you, and still loves you.

Friendship is certainly the finest balm for the pangs of disappointed love.

Jane Austen

If you have one true friend you have more than your share. *Thomas Fuller*

The best type of ships are friendships.

If a friend is in trouble, don't annoy him by asking if there is anything you can do. Think up something appropriate and do it.

Edgar Watson Howe

The best accessories a girl can have are her closest friends. *Paris Hilton*

My friendship it is not in my power to give; this is a gift which no man can make, it is not in our own power: a sound and healthy friendship is the growth of time and circumstance, it will spring up and thrive like a wildflower when these favour, and when they do not, it is in vain to look for it.

William Wordsworth

Sometimes you choose your friends; sometimes they choose you.

He who loses wealth loses much; he who loses a friend loses more; but he that loses his courage, loses all.

Cervantes

I don't like to commit myself about heaven and hell – you see, I have friends in both places.

Mark Twain

Friendship is the perfection of love, and superior to love; it is love purified, exalted, proved by experience, and a consent of minds.
Samuel Richardson

I have always laid it down as a maxim that a man and a woman make far better friendships with the condition that they never have made or are to make love to each other. *Lord Byron*

Sir, more than kisses, letters mingle souls
For thus, friends absent speak.
John Donne

It is wise to apply the oil of refined politeness to the mechanism of friendship.

Colette

To make a friend, be a friend.

Fan the sinking flame of hilarity with the wing of friendship; and pass the rosy wine.

Charles Dickens

Thy friendship oft has made my heart to ache
Do be my enemy – for friendship's sake.
William Blake

Everyone hears what you say. Friends listen to what you say. Best friends understand what you don't say.

Anybody can sympathize with the sufferings of a friend, but it requires a very fine nature to sympathize with a friend's success. *Oscar Wilde*

Love is like the wild-rose briar;
Friendship is like the holly tree.
The holly is dark when the rose briar blooms,
But which will bloom most constantly?

Emily Brontë

A true friend unbosoms freely, advises justly, assists readily, adventures boldly, takes all patiently, defends courageously, and continues a friend unchangeably.
William Penn

True friendship is like sound health; the value of it is seldom known until it be lost.

Charles Caleb Colton

Love is blind. Friendship closes its eyes.

Friedrich Nietzsche

Friendship is the only cement that will ever hold the world together.

Woodrow Wilson

The bird a nest
The spider a web
Man, friendship.

William Blake

When true friends meet in adverse hour
'Tis like a sunbeam through the shower
A watery way an instant seen
The darkly closing clouds between.
Sir Walter Scott

The making of friends, who are real friends, is the best token we have of a man's success in life.

Edward Everett Hale

Friendship without self-interest is one of the rare and beautiful things in life.

James Francis Byrnes

Except in cases of necessity, which are rare, leave your friend to learn unpleasant things from his enemies; they are ready enough to tell them.

Oliver Wendell Holmes

The most beautiful thing we can experience is the mysterious: it is the true source of art, science, and friendship. **Albert Einstein**

A friend should be a master at guessing, and keeping still.

Friedrich Nietzsche

A hedge between Keeps friendships green.

Little do men perceive what solitude is, and how far it extendeth. For a crowd is not company, and faces are but a gallery of pictures, and talk but a tinkling cymbal, where there is no love.

Francis Bacon

A true friend is one who thinks you are a good egg, even if you are half cracked.

It is a sweet thing, friendship, a dear balm
A happy and auspicious bird of calm
Which rides o'er life's ever tumultuous ocean
A God that broods o'er chaos and commotion

Percy Bysshe Shelley

I no doubt deserved my enemies, but I don't believe I deserved my friends.

Walt Whitman

Here's champagne for my real friends, and a real pain for my sham friends. *Francis Bacon*

Friendship must be purchased by friendship. A man can have authority over others, but he can never have their hearts but by giving his own.

Thomas Wilson

True friends are families which you can select.
Audrey Hepburn

Friendship either finds or makes equals.
Publilius Syrus

Friends are lost by calling too often, and calling too seldom. *Scottish proverb*

Friendship is like money, easier made than kept.

Samuel Butler

To be rich in friends is to be poor in nothing.
Lilian Whiting

It is one of the blessings of old friends that you can afford to be stupid with them. *Ralph Waldo Emerson.*

An old friend is a friend to be treasured above all others.

It is more shameful to distrust one's friends than to be deceived by them.

François de La Rochefoucauld

True friendship's laws are by this rule express'd
Welcome the coming, speed the parting guest.

Alexander Pope

In the end, we will remember not the words of our enemies, but the silence of our friends. *Martin Luther King*

Walking with a friend in the dark is better than walking alone in the light. *Helen Keller*

Friendship without self-interest is one of the rare and beautiful things in life.

James Francis Byrnes

When it hurts to look back
And it's hard to look ahead
Look right beside you
And your friend will be there.

Always, sir, set a high value on spontaneous kindness. He whose inclination prompts him to cultivate your friendship of his own accord, will love you more than one whom you have been at pains to attach to you.

Samuel Johnson

A friend is a person with whom I may be sincere. Before him I may think aloud.

Ralph Waldo Emerson

A best friend is like a four-leaf clover:
hard to find, and lucky to have.

**True friendship is a plant
of slow growth and must
undergo and withstand the
shocks of adversity before it
is entitled to the appellation.**
George Washington

Friends are the bacon bits in
the salad bowl of life.

Lose your temper and you lose a friend; lie, and you lose yourself.

Native American proverb

I find friendship to be like wine, raw when new, ripened with age, the true old man's milk and restorative cordial.

Thomas Jefferson

Most of us have a 'best friend' at each stage of life. The luckiest of us have the same one.

The most I can do for my friend is simply to be his friend. I have no wealth to bestow on him. If he knows that I am happy in loving him, he will want no other reward. Is not friendship divine in this?

Henry David Thoreau

The greatest good you can do for another is not just to share your riches but to reveal to him his own.

Benjamin Disraeli

Many people walk in and out of your life, but a true friend leaves footprints on your heart. *Eleanor Roosevelt*

Wherever you are, it's your friends who make your world.
William James

A friend in need is a friend indeed.
Latin proverb

A true friend is one who overlooks your failures and tolerates your success.

Doug Larson

We are all travellers in the wilderness of this world, and the best we can find in our travels is an honest friend.

Robert Louis Stevenson

The best kind of friend is the one you could sit on a porch swing with, never say a word, and come away feeling that was the best conversation you ever had.

Treat your friends as you do your pictures, and place them in the best light.

Winston Churchill

All of us stumble sometimes.
That's why we need a helping hand.

Friendship marks a life even more deeply than love. Love risks degenerating into obsession; friendship is never anything but sharing.

Elie Wiesel

Gratitude preserves old friendships, and procures new.

Friendship is always a sweet responsibility, never an opportunity. *Khalil Gibran*

Of all the things that wisdom acquires to produce the blessedness of the complete life, far the greatest is the possession of friendship. *Epicurus*

The best friends grow together, but can also grow separately without growing apart.

Friendship with oneself is all-important, because without it, one cannot be friends with anybody else in the world. *Eleanor Roosevelt*

Friends are those rare people who ask you how you are, and then wait for the answer.

Let us learn to show our friendship for a man when he is alive, not after he is dead.

F. Scott Fitzgerald

Friendship is the hardest thing in the world to explain. It's not something you learn in school. But if you haven't learned the meaning of friendship, you haven't really learned anything.

Muhammad Ali

A friend is a gift you give yourself.
Robert Louis Stevenson

A friend will accept us as we are, yet help us to be as we should be.

It is one of the severest tests of friendship to tell your friend his faults. So to love a man that you cannot bear to see a stain upon him, and to speak painful truth through loving words, that is friendship. *Henry Ward Beecher*

Love delights in passion; friendship in tranquillity.

Friendship is unnecessary, like philosophy, like art, like the universe itself (for God did not need to create). It has no survival value; rather, it is one of those things that gives value to survival. *C.S. Lewis*

Friendship is like a glass bowl. Once it is broken, it can never be put back together again in exactly the same way.

A single rose can be my garden. A single friend, my world. *Leo Buscaglia*

If it's very painful for you to criticize your friends, you're safe in doing it. But if you take the slightest pleasure in it, that's the time to hold your tongue. *Alice Duer Miller*

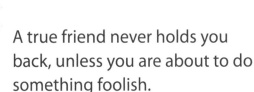

A true friend never holds you back, unless you are about to do something foolish.

Lots of people want to ride with you in the limo, but what you want is someone who will take the bus with you when the limo breaks down.

Oprah Winfrey

A friendship founded on business is better than a business founded on friendship. *John D. Rockefeller*

I have always felt that the great high privilege, relief, and comfort of friendship was that one had to explain nothing.
Katherine Mansfield

A faithful friend is the medicine of life.

The Bible

Fear makes strangers of people who would be friends.

Shirley MacLaine

In everyone's life, at some time our inner fire goes out. It is then burst into flame by an encounter with another human being. We should all be thankful for those people who rekindle the inner spirit.

Albert Schweitzer

Count your years, not with age, but with friends.

True happiness consists not in the multitude of friends, but in their worth and choice. *Samuel Johnson*

Sharing and Caring

What is the secret to long, happy, and devoted friendships? Does it lie in the balance between the two friends, or in the qualities of each? Here, we take a look at how people form friendships, from childhood into adulthood, and what they mean to us as we go through life.

Kindness is the language that the deaf can hear and the blind can see.
Mark Twain

Keep in touch with your friends when they move away, even for good. We never know what twists and turns in life may bring them back to us again.

For a child, choosing and keeping friends is part of the process of growing up and learning how to give and take in a social situation.

Just as romances can blossom in the most surprising circumstances, so too can friendships be forged.

We have two ears and one mouth so we can listen twice as much as we speak. *Epictetus*

We may think ourselves lonely if our friends are far away; but if we have no friends anywhere in the world, that is true loneliness.

Who knows how friendships develop? First, a casual hello; next, perhaps, a chance meeting; and then, often without either person being aware of it, we start to make friends.

We all have a deep desire to be loved, not just by a partner or a family, but by friends.

The bond between humans and animals is a deep one. Most obviously, dogs befriend their masters; but even birds, such as a robin, may fly down and keep a gardener company by perching on a spade while he's digging.

Solitude and friendship are but two aspects of a healthy, well-balanced emotional life.

Friendship is a kind of marriage, and just as liable to divorce.

How many friends do you have? Many, or few? It may be that the fewer you can number, the closer they are to you.

Giving gifts to friends is a way of showing them how much you appreciate them, especially if they are chosen with thought, love, and care.

Be thankful for what you have; you'll end up having more. If you concentrate on what you don't have, you will never, ever have enough. *Oprah Winfrey*

To lose a friend is a great sadness; to gain one, a deep joy.

It's said to be harder to make new friends as you get older. Perhaps. Or could it be that, with the benefit of experience, we become just a little more choosy?

An open, friendly attitude, while enriching our lives, can sometimes lead us to trusting the wrong people. However, being haughty and distrustful is not a sensible alternative, for that way, we may become lonely and embittered.

When did you last make a new friend? If it was a long time ago, perhaps you need to set about making another one… and soon!

We may forgive the mistakes of our friends, but it is unwise to forget them. For by remembering what happened, we learn more about human nature, and, ultimately, about ourselves.

Acquaintances, friends, and family, may greet you with a kiss on the cheek. But only close friends will enfold you in a big hug as well.

When friendships fade, it's easy to cast blame. But sometimes, the relationship has simply run its natural course, and you both need to move on.

Don't be your own worst enemy. Instead, be your own best friend.

We tend to like those who like us; who share opinions, beliefs, common goals, or experience. Sometimes, however, we may find ourselves fascinated by someone completely different.

The way friends run their lives can sometimes seem crazy or stupid; but unless they're harming themselves or others, it's usually best not to be too critical.

All friends disagree. But not all friends argue about their disagreements.

A man's growth is seen in the successive choirs of his friends.
Ralph Waldo Emerson

Friendships are not exempt from the range of negative human emotions, like jealousy, anger, and hatred. Nor are they always free from passionate feelings of love, possessiveness, and obsession.

'Best friends' is a promise, not a label.

Extricating oneself from a friendship that you have outgrown can be a tricky business. If you are not happy, don't allow yourself to be bullied into submission; you have every right to retreat from the relationship, as tactfully and kindly as you can.

A 'frenemy' is a person who smiles to your face, but will stab you in the back given half a chance, by spreading gossip or rumours.

A friend can be a critic, as long as the criticisms obey the rule of the 'three Cs': constructiveness, competence, and concern. First, the criticism should be constructive; second, the friend should know you well enough to be in a position to judge; and third, he or she should care deeply about you.

In friendship, as in marriage, opposites often attract.

Friendships are like helium balloons. Hold on tight to them; for if you let go of them, it's hard to get them back.

Social network sites offer an immediate way of making new friends. But beware: a virtual buddy is no match for a real buddy!

A friend should be one in whose understanding and virtue we can equally confide, and whose opinion we can value at once for its justness and its sincerity.
Robert Hall

In the language of flowers, a gift of red roses speaks of romantic love; pink roses, of affection; and yellow roses, of friendship and devotion.

What makes a friendship?
- Empathy
- Sympathy
- Honesty
- Reciprocity

Research shows that strong, supportive friendships help us to be healthier, as well as happier. In fact, some scientists have called friendship the 'vaccine' that protects both physical and mental health!

Platonic love is a deep, non-romantic friendship between two people of the opposite sex, in which sexual feelings never intrude.

Friends are like rainbows; they come to brighten your life after a storm.

Some friends you have to make an effort to appreciate; others, you simply look forward to spending time with.

Sensitive people are often shy. But that doesn't mean they can't find good friends, usually in a one-to-one situation rather than at social gatherings.

Everyone is both an extravert and an introvert. It just depends on where the balance lies… and which side you show to your friends.

When an acquaintance goes by I often step back from my window, not so much to spare him the effort of acknowledging me as to spare myself the embarrassment of seeing that he has not done so.

Georg Lichtenberg

Two heads are better than one.

Strike up a friendship; strike up the band!

Our old friends are trees that we have planted in the garden of love. Our new friends are flowers that bloom for a summer, and perhaps next year, too.

A best friend is a kind of second self, able to advise and help when the first self is in doubt.

Famous friends in history:
James Madison *and* Thomas Jefferson
Abraham Lincoln *and* Joshua Speed
William 'Bud' Abbot *and* Lou Costello
Gertrude Stein *and* Ernest Hemingway
C.S. Lewis *and* J.R.R. Tolkein
Susan B. Anthony *and* Elizabeth Cady Statton

A large age gap, or other significant difference, is no bar to friendship. For friendship knows no boundaries.

You are never alone when in the company of a good book.

Friendships thrive on social occasions: picnics, parties, dances, discos… or, just as readily, on quiet evenings in, sitting by the fireside and talking.

Even the closest friend doesn't take kindly to bossiness, whether it's in the form of well-meaning advice, or backseat driving.

However much they age, our true friends always look beautiful to us – just as we hope to look beautiful to them.

The two great companions of a lifetime are friendship and learning.

Over sixty-five per cent of young children have 'imaginary friends'. These 'friends' can be anything from a flying penguin to a tiny baby, and playing games with them is a normal part of a child's development.

To read the wit and wisdom of the ancients is to make friends with the past.

I live with her in the beauty of peace and of all delights and sweetness. I am directed by her counsels, supported by her prayers. I press forward by her merits, I am upheld by her kindnesses, and daily, I enjoy conversation with her. *Guibert of Gembloux regarding Hildegard of Bingen*

Allow your children to choose their own friends. If you worry that they'll be a bad influence, try just keeping an eye on the situation, rather than intervening.

Cooking for friends can be a great pleasure. It doesn't have to be a fancy meal – a large pot of stew, a hearty soup, a crusty loaf, and a bottle of wine, is feast enough.

A difficult time can sometimes seem hilarious afterwards – especially if you have old friends to laugh about it with.

When a cat adopts you, there is nothing to be done about it except put up with it, until the wind changes.

T. S. Eliot

People need friends the most when they deserve them the least.

You cannot be successful without making enemies, as well as friends.

Be the change you want to see in the world.

Mahatma Gandhi

We learn much from our own mistakes; and more from our friends' mistakes.

We are not human beings on a spiritual journey; we are spiritual beings on a human journey.

Teilhard de Chardin

There are those who pass like ships in the night
Who meet for a moment, then sail out of sight.
With never a backward glance of regret
Folks we know briefly, then quickly forget.
But the truest of friends sail on together
Through still, calm waters and stormy weather
Helping each other through joy and through strife
These are the friends who give meaning to life.

Friendship, like love, is a kind of recognition, soul to soul.

By friendship you mean the greatest love, the greatest usefulness, the most open communication, the noblest sufferings, the severest truth, the heartiest counsel, and the greatest union of minds of which brave men and women are capable.
Jeremy Taylor

You know you have a friend when he or she is happy for your success in life, whether or not your future includes them.

Ancient
Wisdom

In classical times, friendship seems to have occupied a central place in the lives of great thinkers, possibly because most of them were men, and women were regarded, on the whole, as inferior beings, rather than equal companions (with a few notable exceptions). Here is a selection of their writings on the subject, which are as thought-provoking today as when they were first written.

The antidote for fifty enemies is one friend. *Aristotle*

Have no friends not equal to yourself. *Confucius*

Nothing but heaven itself is better than a friend who is really a friend.

Plautus

Only your friends will tell you when your face is dirty.

Spanish proverb

Never injure a friend, even in jest.

Cicero

A troublemaker plants seeds of strife; gossip separates the best of friends.
The Bible

Give and take makes good friends.

One who looks for a friend without faults will have none.
Jewish proverb

A true friend wants nothing more from you than the pleasure of your company.

It is not so much our friends' help that helps us, as the confident knowledge that they will help us.
Epictetus

He who walks with the wise grows wise, but a companion of fools suffers harm.

The Bible

The wise man remembers his friend at all times; the fool, only when he has need of them.

There is nothing on this earth more to be prized than true friendship.

Thomas Aquinas

Never be friends with a man who is not better than yourself. **Confucius**

Friends and wine should be old.

The friendship that can cease has never been real.
Saint Jerome

What is a friend? A single soul dwelling in two bodies.
Aristotle

Greater love hath no man than this, that he lay down his life for his friend. *The Bible*

A friend is someone who knows the song in your heart, and can sing it back to you when you have forgotten the words.

A quarrel between friends, when made up, adds a new tie to friendship.
Saint Francis de Sales

Kindness gives birth to kindness.

Sophocles

Better to weep with wise men than to laugh with fools.

I don't need a friend who changes when I change, and who nods when I nod; my shadow does that much better.

Plutarch

To like and dislike the same things, that indeed is the true friendship.
Sallust

One loyal friend is worth ten thousand relatives.
Euripides

Between true friends, even shared water tastes sweet. *Chinese proverb*

Good friends are the most important ingredient in the recipe for a long and happy life.

Friendship is the only thing in the world concerning the usefulness of which all mankind are agreed.

Cicero

Silence is the true friend that never betrays.

Friendship is a slow ripening fruit.

Aristotle

Be slow to fall into friendship,
but when you are in, continue
firm and constant. **Socrates**

Hold a true friend with both your hands.
Nigerian proverb

Misfortune shows those who are not true friends.

Aristotle

Nature has no love for solitude, and always leans, as it were, on some support; and the sweetest support is to be found in the most intimate friendship. *Cicero*

Friends have all things in common.

Plato

Money may make you wealthy, but a true friend makes you rich.

Without friends no one would choose to live, though he had all other goods.

Aristotle

Friendship redoubleth joys, and cutteth grief in half.

Francis Bacon

If we should forgive our enemies, how much more important it is that we should forgive our friends.

Tell me what company thou keepest, and I'll tell thee what thou art. *Cervantes*

A person standing alone can be attacked and defeated, but two can stand back-to-back and conquer. Three are even better, for a triple-braided cord is not easily broken.

The Bible

Don't let the grass grow on the path to friendship.

Indian proverb

A friend is one to whom one can pour out all the contents of one's heart, chaff and grain together, knowing that the gentlest of hands will take and sift it, keeping what is worth keeping, and, with the breath of kindness, blowing the rest away. *Arab proverb*

Life is nothing without friendship.

Cicero

Friendship is the only cure for hatred, the only guarantee of peace. *Buddha*

A friend is, as it were, a second self.
Cicero

True friendship is self-love at second hand.
William Hazlitt

If two friends ask you to judge a dispute, do not accept, because you will lose one of them; on the other hand, if two strangers come to you with the same request, accept, because you will gain one friend.

St Augustine

It is better to be in a prison with friends than in a garden with strangers.

A friend to all is a friend to none.
Aristotle

A friend is someone who walks in when the world has walked out.

Prayer is nothing more than being on terms of friendship with God. *St Teresa of Avila*

An insincere and evil friend is more to be feared than a wild beast; a wild beast may wound your body, but an evil friend will wound your mind.

Buddha

With clothes, the newest are best; with friends, the oldest are best.

Chinese proverb

May there always be work for your hands to do;
May your purse always hold a coin or two;
May the sun always shine on your windowpane;
May a rainbow be certain to follow each rain;
May the hand of a friend always be near you;
May God fill your heart with gladness and cheer.

Irish rhyme

One who knows how to show and accept kindness will be a better friend than any.

Sophocles

Make friends with the angels, who though invisible are always with you. Often invoke them, constantly praise them, and make good use of their help and assistance in all your temporal and spiritual affairs.

Saint Francis de Sales

True friendship ought never to conceal what it thinks.

Saint Jerome

Many a time from bad beginnings have true friendships sprung.

Terence

Friendship is not only a question of choice; it is also, in part, a question of circumstance.

Real friendship is shown in times of trouble; prosperity is full of friends.

Euripides

A tree is known by its fruit; a man by his deeds. A good deed is never lost; he who sows courtesy reaps friendship, and he who plants kindness gathers love. *St Basil*

The Test of Time

Having a few loyal, close friends is one of the greatest blessings life can offer. How can we show our appreciation, if we have friends; and if we don't, how can we learn from our mistakes, and start to build positive relationships in our lives?

When life gets you down, it's good to have a friend around.

Friends don't always need advice; they may just want a listening ear, or a shoulder to cry on.

A loyal friend is a true companion for life.

Interests in common are a good basis for friendship. But sometimes a friend who has different interests from you can introduce you to a whole new world that you never knew existed.

They say that schooldays are the best of your life. That may not be true for everyone, but school friends are certainly the ones you'll remember for the rest of your life!

False friends are worse than bitter enemies. *Scottish proverb*

Making friends with a person from a different country, culture, or social background can be an enriching and enlivening experience, giving us a new perspective on our lives.

Whenever you're in conflict with someone, there is one factor that can make the difference between damaging your relationship and deepening it. That factor is attitude.
William James

Be a friend to yourself: be that quiet voice beside you. Advise yourself; encourage yourself; and, when you feel anxious and afraid, calm yourself.

Unburdening yourself to a friend is one of the best ways to fight the blues. But you'll need to be prepared to do the same for your friend, listening to their tale of woe, too, when their turn comes.

With a good friend beside you, you can brave all the disasters life can bring.

If you become angry with your friend, for whatever reason, there are several ways to deal with the situation. You can keep your distance for a little while, hoping your anger will simmer down; you can keep seeing each other and try to control your anger when you're together; or you can quietly and calmly tell them how you feel, so that the conflict can begin to be resolved.

Seeing a friendship blossom is like watching a flower grow.

Don't envy other people's close friendships – use them as an example for your own.

To laugh often and much; to win the respect of intelligent people and the affection of children; to earn the appreciation of honest critics and to endure the betrayal of false friends; to appreciate beauty; to find the best in others; to leave this world a bit better whether by a healthy child, a garden patch, or a redeemed social condition; to know even one life has breathed easier because you have lived. This is to have succeeded.

Ralph Waldo Emerson

Our friends provide us with an escape from the responsibilities of our family and domestic lives. With them, we can laugh about the things that drive us crazy at home!

Nobody really understands what brings two people together in a friendship. Perhaps it's a kind of magic…

Stick up for your friends when other people talk about them behind their backs. Hopefully, they'll do the same for you.

Lasting friendships are built one day at a time.

Sometimes friends discuss the problems of another friend together. Usually, this is a helpful thing to do, but sometimes it can degenerate into gossip. Be careful not to say too much – gossip has a way of getting back to the person who's the centre of it, and can be the cause of much conflict between friends.

When a woman like that whom I've seen so much
All of a sudden drops out of touch
Is always busy, and never can
Spare you a moment
It means a man.

Alice Duer Miller

A colleague at work can become a trusted friend. He or she will understand, better than most partners, the pressures of the workplace, and how relationships there shift and change.

The problem with friendships at work is that, often, the environment is extremely competitive. Only when you are sure you can trust your colleagues, can you be friends with them. And being friends with the boss is even more difficult!

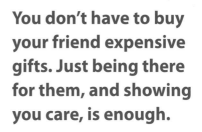

You don't have to buy your friend expensive gifts. Just being there for them, and showing you care, is enough.

I get by with a little help from my friends.

John Lennon

We are all leaves on the tree of friendship.

A fair-weather friend is one who is only your friend when circumstances are pleasant or profitable. These are the friends who will desert you at the first sign of trouble.

All of us have different levels of friendship in our lives. First, there are our close friends, who may only number one or two. Then there are our 'social friends' or work colleagues, a wider circle whom we know and care for, but would not trust with our intimate secrets. Finally, there are our acquaintances, people we come into contact with regularly, but do not know well. This last group of people always have the potential to become friends.

There are three faithful friends in life: an old wife, an old dog, and ready money.

Benjamin Franklin

The six signs of a healthy friendship:
- You can be honest with each other
- You can argue, gently and with humour
- You can encourage other friendships
- You can trust each other implicitly
- You can respect each other's boundaries
- You both take time and care to nurture the relationship

Your child is not your friend. However close your relationship with your child, keep in mind that you must function as a parent, not a friend. In particular, don't confide in your child, who will not be emotionally mature enough to deal with your problems.

It's sad when a friend forgets us, and moves on. But sometimes we have to accept that is the case, and move on too.

The intimacy of close friendship is something that certain people find hard to cope with. Respect that in your friend, but slowly, through trust, try to change it.

Sometimes friendships that flourish within the context of work flounder outside it. It may be that you can make friends with someone very different from you within a work environment, but not find much in common outside it.

You can't stay in your corner of the forest waiting for others to come to you. You have to go to them sometimes. *Winnie the Pooh*

Taking holidays together can be quite a strain on friendships. Before you leave, find out what each expects from the other, and build in time, if necessary, that you spend apart.

Sometimes we make friends with people who don't like each other. In that situation, don't force them together. Respect their differences, and leave it at that.

List your friends. Then think about what you have done for each one of them lately. If not much, it's time to make amends!

Be nice to the people you meet going up, because you're sure to meet them again on your way down.

Jimmy Durante

Keeping up friendships takes time and effort, but that time and effort is never wasted.

Friendship is a matter of deep respect, rather than superficial politeness.

Friends can guide you; friends can chide you; but best of all, is a friend beside you.

It's important simply to relax and wind down sometimes – to go out for a meal or a drink, to the cinema, or to watch a ball game. And who better to do that with than a close friend?

If you knew everything your friends were thinking about you, they probably wouldn't be your friends!

If you're tired and fed up, you may want to retreat into your home. A true friend is someone you can retreat with, someone you don't have to put up a front for.

Ceremony was but devised at first
To set a gloss on faint deeds, hollow welcomes,
Recanting goodness, sorry 'ere 'tis shown
But where there is true friendship
There needs none.

William Shakespeare

Be honest; be reliable; be kind; be caring; laugh often. Nothing more is needed in a friend.

Try to see yourself through your friends' eyes from time to time; you may see yourself differently if you do.

Often, old friends never seem to look old to us. That may be because they have remained young at heart; or because we, too, have aged, and can't see it in them or ourselves.

Devotion to a best friend must be absolute and unconditional.

Friendship is not just about privilege; it's also about duty.

At what point does an acquaintance become a friend? Usually, when the two of you have undergone some bonding experience together, whether pleasant or unpleasant.

Friends sometimes need to be left alone. And sometimes, they need to be coaxed out of their shells. Knowing what is needed, and acting on it at the right time, is an important part of friendship.

If you lose a friend and it causes you pain, look back on what you did wrong. Perhaps you were too egocentric; perhaps too impatient; or perhaps the two of you were just incompatible. Whatever the reason, try to learn from what has happened, and avoid doing it again.

A bond between close friends is altogether different from that between 'social' friends.

The face of a friend is like a picture in a locket that you carry close to your heart.

Nowadays, we seldom write letters. Mobile phones and emails quickly put us in touch with our friends. But now and again, perhaps on a birthday or at Christmas, it's nice to write a proper letter to a friend far away… and hopefully, to receive one back.

Some people go through life with a best friend, which is a wonderful relationship to have. But many of us, after childhood, don't have 'best friends', or at least, don't call them that. Instead, if we're lucky we have a 'special' or 'close' friend.

Do you sometimes take an instant liking to a person and think, 'I'd like to make friends with you'? If so, think about how you can do so without seeming pushy… perhaps, initially, by inviting them out to some kind of group function like a concert or party.

Men kick around friendship like a football, but it doesn't seem to crack.
Women treat it like glasses, and it goes to pieces.

Anne Morrow Lindbergh

Going round to a friend's, sitting in the kitchen over a cup of tea or coffee, and chatting about what's going on in each other's lives, is an ordinary but important pleasure in life.

Love, love, love: that is friendship.

Bring your friends together through parties, dinners, and other social occasions. It will be fun for them, and it helps to build a supportive circle around you.

There is a scarcity of friendship, but not of friends. *Thomas Fuller*

If you feel down, don't be afraid to tell a friend. But make sure that when they feel the same way, you are there for them, too.

Life is not easy for any of us; that's something you learn when you have a close friend, and begin to understand the problems in their lives as well as your own.

Don't feel you have to measure up to a friend's flair for entertaining. Think about what kind of social event you enjoy, and invite your friends to join you. That way, you won't be being competitive – you'll just be being you.

It is rare to remain in touch with a childhood friend throughout life; but when it happens, it is a great joy.

Life without friends is dull, lonely, and harsh. Life with them is fun, companionable, and a great deal happier.

Many people have difficulties feeling at ease in social situations, such as parties. Instead, involve yourself in activities you enjoy, and you may find, when the pressure's off to look your best or make small talk, you can begin to relax and be yourself.

Love between friends is the easiest kind of love. The passion of romantic love, the intensity of emotion between parent and child, is often far more fraught and complex.

The ultimate measure of a person is not where they stand in moments of comfort and convenience, but where they stand in times of challenge and controversy.

Martin Luther King

A problem shared is a problem halved.

A long chat on the phone … a card congratulating you on a small success in your life … dropping round for tea on a rainy Sunday afternoon … these are the little things that, with friends, mean so much.

You don't need to tattoo the name of a friend on to your body; your mind will always carry the image … and it won't fade, either!

Time makes friendship mellow.

Kindness is the greatest of human virtues, and who better to be kind to than your friends?

In times of bereavement, some turn to religion; others to art, or travel. But most of all, we turn to our friends.

Friendship is like a silken thread; tough, but delicate. Take care not to break it.

The way to love anything is to realize that it might be lost.

G.K. Chesterton

Money and friendship don't mix. Don't borrow money from your friends, and don't lend it either, unless you can be sure you won't fall out over it.

Sometimes a friend tests our patience to the point where we may consider breaking off the relationship. We should think carefully before we do; friendships take time to build, and their loss will be felt deeply once they are gone.

Friends will help you out in a crisis; but make sure you don't have too many crises, or they may become weary of your demands for help.

Small acts of kindness have a way of being repaid with kindness.

Life is a complicated operation – friendship acts as the anaesthetic.

At times our own light goes out and is rekindled by a spark from another person. Each of us has cause to think with deep gratitude of those who have lighted the flame within us.

Albert Schweitzer

A friend is a person who helps you to become what you truly are.

True friends do not flatter; but they are eager to praise when praise is due.

Even the best of friends can be jealous of each other sometimes. Don't be ashamed of your jealousy; recognize the feeling as part of human nature, then let it pass.

To me, fair friend, you never can be old
For as you were when first your eye I eyed
Such seems your beauty still.

William Shakespeare

A true friend takes pleasure in our talents and strengths; a false friend pretends to.

If your friend annoys you sometimes, try to be patient; and think about how much worse it would be if you had no friend.

Think twice before burdening a friend with a secret. *Marlene Dietrich*

I may have no country; I may have no job;
I may have no money; I may have no family.
But if I have no friend, I am truly poor.

When you become successful, it's suprising how many friends come out of the woodwork. Enjoy being the centre of attention, but don't let it go to your head. Because if things change, those fair-weather friends won't be seen for dust.

Circumstances sometimes bring two people together for a brief period, and when those circumstances change, they drift apart. That doesn't mean the friendship is not valuable or significant; only that its time has come and gone.

Going on holiday alone, or with a friend? Eating dinner by yourself, or with a friend? Most of us would choose the latter option, wouldn't we?

When trouble knocks at your friend's door, go and join the queue.

A friend is someone you can talk things over with, knowing you can trust them to keep your secrets safe.

The familiar voice of an old friend is a welcome sound, especially in times of trouble and distress.

Do you know someone who is going through a hard time? Let them know you are thinking of them – it will mean a lot to them.

There is nothing better than the encouragement of a good friend.

Katherine Hathaway

If you look after your friends, chances are, they'll look after you.

Friendship takes time and trouble. In today's busy world, we may feel that we can't afford the extra input – but, if we can find the time, we're sure to be richly rewarded.

Kindness is never wasted on a friend.

In life's trials and tribulations, it is to our friends that we look for comfort and reassurance.

Family and friends must rank highest on our list of priorities.

Friendship is a soothing balm to the soul.

The deepest craving of human nature is to be appreciated.
William James

A dog is the most faithful companion you'll ever have. Always pleased to see you; always happy to be in your company; always sad to see you go.

Friends are a great comfort in times of trouble; but they're also a great delight in times of joy.

What is a friend, if not an equal?

The trouble with most of us is that we would rather be ruined by praise than saved by criticism.

Norman Vincent Peale

Getting to know friends, in all their uniqueness as human beings, is one of the sweetest pleasures of life.

Best friends don't always need to be present; they can keep you company in your heart.

Caring and sharing; that's what friendship's all about.

He is a wise man who does not grieve for the things he has not, but rejoices for those which he has. *Epictetus*

Sometimes, people expect too much of their friends. Remember… nobody's perfect!

**You have troubles. Your friend has them too.
So stick together, and decide what to do.**

We can only be said to be alive in those moments when our hearts are conscious of our treasures.

Thornton Wilder

It's said that cats are solitary animals; but, in fact, they tend to bond in pairs, rather than packs, and often seek out the presence of human beings.

A true friend will:
Touch your heart with kindness
Make you double up with laughter
Know when to offer advice
Understand when to remain silent.

You may find your friends odd and quirky. They may think the same about you. But that's all part of the fun!

Forgive many things in others; nothing in yourself.

Aldous Huxley

It takes time and patience to build a friendship. In the beginning, don't be too needy. Wait until you know the person well before talking about your intimate problems.

Cultivate the habit of gratitude. Write a gratitude diary, listing all the things that bring you joy in life, including your friends.

Holidays are a great time to celebrate friendship, with thoughtful cards, gifts, and social occasions.

Going to a new school or college, moving house, changing one's job. All these are situations in which we have to make new friends. Go into them with an open-minded attitude. Wait for social invitations – and if they don't come, be the first to make them.

When a person is seriously ill, the unwavering support and help of a friend can make all the difference in the world.

Clear boundaries between work and friendship are needed, so that our duties and loyalties in each situation are clear.

Let us be grateful to the people who make us happy. They are the charming gardeners who make our souls blossom. *Marcel Proust*

Friends for Life

The blossoming of a friendship is often a mystery, as people who are quite different – almost opposite, perhaps – in nature may form a close bond. Here, we take a look at this phenomenon, and ask how we can teach our children, and ourselves, the value of friendship.

Friendship leaves a footprint on the heart.

A real friend is someone you imagine will still be there when you grow old.

However rare true love may be, it is less so than friendship.

Albert Einstein

We may call many people friends; but how many can we confidently say are our true friends?

In order to keep a friendship, we must be prepared to make allowances for our friend, overlooking what we don't like, and valuing what we do.

True friends are like diamonds – bright, beautiful, valuable, and always in style.

Nicole Richie

Walking and talking, and taking in nature's beauty all the while, is one of friendship's great delights.

If you always have to be careful what you say to your friends, for fear they may pass on gossip, then they're not your true friends.

In the long term, our friends will be far more valuable to us than our possessions.

The companions of our childhood always possess a certain power over our minds which hardly any later friend can obtain. *Mary Shelley*

True friends feel your pain as if it were their own.

When we are angry with our friends, it is often because they remind us of our own faults.

Never worry alone – find a friend to share your fears with, and you will find comfort and reassurance.

Love is a friendship with erotic moments.
Antonio Gala

Friends owe each other nothing but love and loyalty.

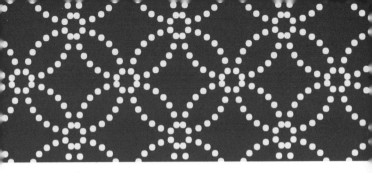

Have you ever watched two friends talk – the way they copy each other's gestures, as if each were a reflection of the other?

Love is friendship set to music.

Jackson Pollock

Friendships change like the seasons: coming to life in spring, blossoming in summer, fading in autumn, dormant in winter… and then renewing themselves again…

It takes two to tango.

Plain food cooked by friends who love you may taste better than fancy food in a restaurant.

Give me the man that is not passion's slave
And I will wear him in my heart's core
As I do thee.

William Shakespeare

Sometimes, in old age, a rift between old friends is healed. For, in the long term, we would rather have a friend than consider ourselves in the right.

With friends, we feel we don't have to explain, because we both speak the same language.

Be a friend to thyself, and others will be so too.
Thomas Fuller

All friends get a little jealous
of each other sometimes.
However, beware the friends
who are too jealous, for they
are blinded by envy and truly
cannot love you.

In this divine glass they see face to face; and their converse is free, as well as pure. This is the comfort of friends, that though they may be said to die, yet their friendship and society are, in the best sense, ever present, because immortal.

William Penn

Value friendship while it is yours; otherwise, you may only realize how important it is when it's gone.

When twilight drops her curtain down
And pins it with a star
Remember that you have a friend
Though she may wander far.
L.M. Montgomery

Don't be afraid to disagree with your friends for fear of offending them. No one wants a friend who agrees with everything they say.

Dressing up when you go out to dinner with friends shows respect for your host; and besides that, it's fun!

In a sense, you owe your friends nothing. But in another sense, you owe them everything.

Human beings are born into this little span of life of which the best thing is its friendships and intimacies … and yet they leave their friendships and intimacies with no cultivation, to grow as they will by the roadside …

William James

True friends don't try to change us, unless we want to change ourselves.

When you have achieved a success in life, make sure to thank the friends who have helped you. There are sure to be some, and they are sure to appreciate your thanks.

The shifts of fortune test the reliability of friends. *Cicero*

When people lose friends in death, they may often dream about them, and thus give themselves the chance to talk to their dear ones again, face to face.

Friendships don't necessarily make you happy. But they should provide great comfort and companionship when you're feeling sad.

For no one, in our long decline
So dusty, spiteful, and divided
Had quite such pleasant friends as mine
Or loved them half as much as I did.

Hilaire Belloc

When people ask, 'How are you?', we usually reply, 'Fine', however we're feeling. But when close friends ask, you can tell them the truth, because you know they really care.

The more you get to know your friends, the more peculiar you may find them. But the strange thing is, the more you start to love their peculiarities.

What an exotic visitor you have here, in this household friend, the cat who purrs as you stroke, or rub his chin, or scratch his head.

Doris Lessing

After a sad event such as a bereavement or failure, a true friend can make life worth living once again.

I have unclasped to thee the book Even of my secret soul.

William Shakespeare

We love our families, but we don't necessarily like them; the same is not usually true of our friends, whom we both like and love.

When a marriage ends in divorce, what both parties may miss most is the common bond of friendship that once existed between them.

For I hope my friends will pardon me, when I declare, I know none of them without a fault; and I should be sorry if I could imagine, I had any friend who could not see mine. Forgiveness, of this kind, we give and demand in turn.

Henry Fielding

Have you ever had two friends in a room, and begun to realize you are two different people to these two friends? It's an uncomfortable feeling, and one that we all recognize.

If you are unhappy with yourself, you are likely to find fault with your friends.

Isn't that what matters? To have someone who can remember with you? To have someone who remembers how far you've come?

Judy Blume

Do not mourn too long when friends die. They would prefer us to remember the happy times we had with them, rather than dwell on the sadness of the parting.

Children go to school to be educated – and to make friends, which is a lifelong education in itself.

True friendship resists time, distance, and silence. *Isabel Allende*

Sometimes, a friendship is based on a shared ideal between two people, who go out together to face the world, in the hopes that their vision will become a reality.

My friendships, they are a very strong part of my life, they are as light as gossamer but also they are as strong as steel… I love them at the point where they say: It is nice to see you again. And I love them too at the point when they say: Good-bye, come again soon. The rhythm of friendship is a very good rhythm.

Stevie Smith

Friendship is about giving support, rather than advice.

Those who are going nowhere can have no fellow-travellers. *C.S. Lewis*

Male friends watch sports together; female friends chat on the telephone. A stereotype perhaps, but one with more than a little truth in it.

Close friends are truly life's treasures. Sometimes they know us better than we know ourselves. With gentle honesty, they are there to guide and support us, to share our laughter and our tears. Their presence reminds us that we are never really alone.

Vincent Van Gogh

Everyone needs friends, even those who say they don't.

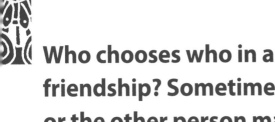

Who chooses who in a friendship? Sometimes, one or the other person makes the first move. But often, it's rather hard to say!

Maybe being married is talking to oneself with one's other self listening.
Ruth Rendell

A Friend
Indeed

Recent research has shown that being able to talk to a friend about personal problems has important mental health benefits. It has also revealed that most people have fewer than five friends that they consider close. So having a small number of close friends turns out to be the key to a balanced, happy, healthy, life.

With a good friend, you smile a little more often; anger a little less quickly. The sun shines a little brighter; and life is a little sweeter.

Some friendships withstand the test of time; others, sadly, fail it.

It's the friends you can call up at 4 a.m. that matter.

Marlene Dietrich

Friendship is part of a long, happy marriage in which both partners like, as well as love, one another.

Friendship is one of the most important gifts we can ever offer another human being.

Good friends, good books, and a sleepy conscience: this is the ideal life.
Mark Twain

In many cases, friendships are formed through shared interests or through working together, and may overcome big differences of personality and social background.

There is nothing better than a friend, unless it is a friend with chocolate.

Charles Dickens

You don't need to keep explaining yourself. Your friends already understand you, and your enemies won't be interested.

Good friends are like the stars in the sky; you can't always see them, but you know they're there.

Words are easy, like the wind
Faithful friends are hard to find.

William Shakespeare

Your best friend will
tell you what you
don't want to know.

Love is blind, but friendship is kind.

It is not a lack of love, but a lack of friendship that makes unhappy marriages.

Friedrich Nietzsche

You meet by chance; you become friends by choice.

Where do we make friends? At school, at college, at work, through other friends… anywhere and everywhere.

An honest answer is the true sign of friendship.

There is nothing I would not do for those who are really my friends. I have no notion of loving people by halves, it is not my nature. *Jane Austen*

A best friend is someone you can tell your hopes and dreams to and know they won't laugh.

Life is what we make it; and part of what we make it is the friends we choose.

When it hurts to look back, and you're scared to look ahead, it helps if you can look right beside you and find a friend.

If I had a flower for every time I thought of you, I could walk through my garden forever.

Alfred Lord Tennyson

Friendship is a gift for when your spirits need a lift!

Most people are not important enough to have enemies; but we are all important enough to have friends.

Friends are part of the glue that holds life and faith together.

Jon Katz

Friendships sometimes depend on circumstance. It is only when our paths have crossed several times that we may decide to become friends.

A true friend is someone who likes you and doesn't want anything from you.

There is no surer foundation for a beautiful friendship than a mutual taste in literature.

P. G. Wodehouse

First impressions can be wrong, but more often, they are right.

When you grow up side by side with a friend, your roots are tangled together... even when you grow apart.

If you want to make friends, don't try to impress people with how interesting you are. Instead, listen to them, and find out how interesting they are.

The best way to destroy an enemy is to make him a friend.

Abraham Lincoln

Friendship is a matter of timing.
A time to reach out; a time to hold
back; a time to advise; a time to
keep silent; and a time to pick up the
pieces when the trouble's over.

The friend who holds your hand and says the wrong thing is made of dearer stuff than the one who stays away.

Barbara Kingsolver

Some people are loners. They prefer to live separately from others. But however independent they are, most of them would probably warm to a friend.

Being a friend is a statement of hope and faith.

Those who are far from home, without family around them, know best the value of true friends.

No friendship is an accident.
O. Henry

Friendship is based on truth, not lies.

When a friendship begins, we notice everything that we have in common. When it ends, we realize how different we have been, all along.

A good writer possesses not only his own spirit, but the spirit of his friends. *Friedrich Nietzsche*

With friends, whatever the differences in our experience of life, we feel a sense that we have all come from the same place.

Real friends don't mind if, when they call, your house is in a mess. They've come to see you, not your house!

Constant use had not worn ragged the fabric of their friendship.

Dorothy Parker

When you're feeling down about yourself, a friend can remind you of your talents, skills, and everything else that's good about you.

Even in the midst of an exciting new romance, don't forget to keep in touch with your friends. They will be there for you when the excitement is over.

Feeling that one is loved by a friend gives one a great sense of value, happiness, and comfort in life.

The best relationships – the ones that last – are the ones that are rooted in friendship.

Gillian Anderson

When you meet the person who will become your friend in life, there is often a sense of recognition. Not always immediately, though; that may come later...

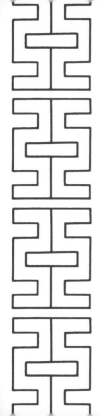

Even the best of friends must allow each other a measure of privacy. If they can't, the friendship becomes intrusive.

I ask you to judge me by the enemies I have made.

Franklin D. Roosevelt

Everyone needs a person they can talk to about their innermost feelings. That could be a partner, but often, it's a friend, who is not caught up in the web of family relationships around us.

Your closest friends see not only what you are, but what you could be.

I don't trust people who say they have a lot of friends. It's a sure sign that they don't really know anyone.

Carlos Ruiz Zafon

A best friend is the person who understands you better than you understand yourself.

Your creative life is a kind of friend you can spend time with whenever you like: whether writing, painting, or playing music. It's somewhere to go where you will always be welcomed.

A friend is someone to complain to about life's little irritations – but make sure you let them complain as well!

Friendships are a little like love affairs. If they happen too quickly, they may pass just as quickly. If they grow slowly, they may last longer.

A friend may be waiting behind a stranger's face.

Maya Angelou

Sometimes when we meet a person for the first time, he or she feels like an old friend. That's a good omen for a true friendship.